How Your Pet Grows!

Hoppy the Toad

Jane Burton

Random House 🏠 New York

Library of Congress Cataloging-in-Publication Data:
Burton, Jane. Hoppy the toad. (How your pet grows!) SUMMARY: Text and photographs describe how a toad changes from a tadpole to a toadlet to a toad during its first three years of life and how it eats, hibernates, and spawns. ISBN: 0-394-82270-6 (pbk.); 0-394-92270-0 (lib. bdg.) 1. Toads as pets—Juvenile literature. 2. Toads —Development—Juvenile literature. [1. Toads] I. Title. II. Series: Burton, Jane. How your pet grows! SF459.T54B87 1989 639.3'787 89-42690

Manufactured in Hong Kong   1 2 3 4 5 6 7 8 9 0

Toads are spawning in the big pond. A female toad lays her eggs in jelly-like strings—called "spawn"—as she swims along.

Each little black blob in the spawn is an egg. Soon it starts to grow a head and a tail. In a few days it begins to squirm and uncurl. Hoppy, the first little tadpole, wriggles until she swims out of the jelly.

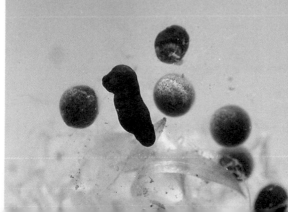

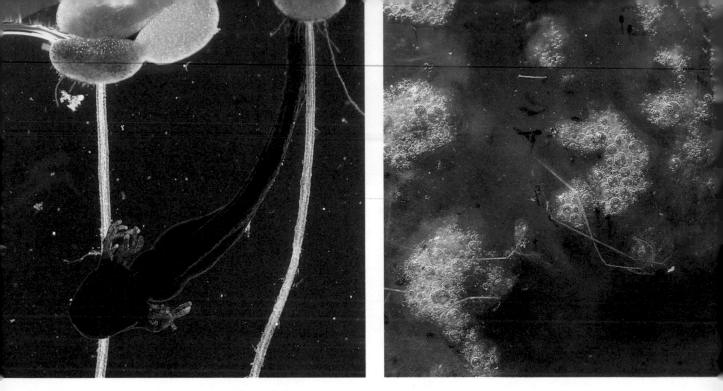

One week old

Now Hoppy has a long tail for swimming. She breathes through the feathery gills on each side of her head. She swims away from the old jelly and attaches herself to a duckweed stem.

Three weeks old

The tadpoles are feeding in algae, which makes air bubbles in the sun. The bubbles lift the algae out of the water and Hoppy almost gets stuck. She struggles to swim away.

Four weeks old

A cover of skin has grown over Hoppy's gills.
She can swim really fast by fluttering her tail.
All the tadpoles stay near the surface in a big
group called a school.

Eight weeks old

The tadpoles have grown hind legs. Front legs
are growing too. They will pop out of the bulge
forming at the gill covers. Soon the tadpoles
won't need their gills because they will start to
breathe air through their nostrils.

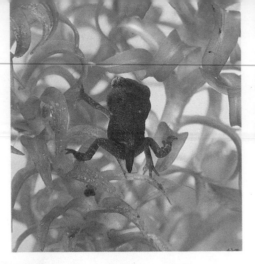

Twelve weeks old

Hoppy is no longer a tadpole. Now she is nearly a toadlet. She has stopped eating and is living off the food energy stored in her tail. As her body grows, her tail gets smaller and smaller.

Sixteen weeks old

One damp day after a thunderstorm, all the toadlets climb out of the pond and crawl away to begin their life on land.

Hoppy battles through a "forest" of moss stems. The stems are not really very tall, but she is very tiny.

Five months old

Each night during the summer, Hoppy crawls around looking for tiny insects to snap up. She is growing fast all the time. Little by little she travels farther away from the big pond.

Six months old

Hoppy reaches the woods where Warty lives. Warty is a grown-up toad. He watches Hoppy as if he might eat her. Hoppy stays very still. Warty needs to see his prey move before deciding to snap it up. Hoppy doesn't move, so Warty loses interest and crawls on.

Like toads, snails only come out into the open when it is cool and damp. So Hoppy and Sam the snail are out one day after a rainstorm.

Sam has been eating a toadstool. Now he starts to glide away, waving his eyes, which are on the ends of stalks. Hoppy notices the movement of an eyestalk and gets ready to snap at it. It could be something to eat.

Sam does not seem to notice Hoppy as he glides toward her. Hoppy puts up a foot and shoves the snail in the face. Sam quickly draws in his eyestalks to protect his delicate eyes. Hoppy starts to creep away, for there is no food here, just the snail. Suddenly Sam's eyes zoom out again and he lands right on top of Hoppy by mistake. Snails eat only vegetables, so Hoppy is in no danger and slips away unharmed.

Eight months old

Hoppy is a "cold-blooded" animal—her body is always the same temperature as the ground and air. In the summer she is lively, but now that winter is coming, Hoppy is too cold to eat. She moves more slowly, and her skin turns black.

Before she gets so cold that she cannot move at all, Hoppy finds a safe place in which to "hibernate," or rest for the winter. She crawls into a hole under a log. Snails are already gathered there.

Hoppy and the snails go into hibernation. They are not exactly asleep but their bodies "shut down." They don't eat or move, and they hardly breathe. They stay this way all through the hard winter weather.

In the spring, the sun warms the ground again. Hoppy and the snails soon come creeping out of hibernation.

Eighteen months old

All through her second summer Hoppy is hardly seen at all. During the day she stays in a damp place under a log. She only comes out at night, when it is cool and damp.

At the end of the summer a storm blows all the leaves off the trees. It rains and rains until the ground is waterlogged. A toad must have dampness, but it hates a flood!

Hoppy is washed out of her home and has to swim. She climbs out of the water onto a little island. Perched on the edge, she looks out across a huge puddle. Suddenly the "island" rocks slightly, then starts to move.

The "island" turns around! A sharp nose pokes out of it, and an eye appears. A head rises from the water. Hoppy backs away. The turtle untucks its feet and paddles across the puddle, carrying Hoppy to the far side.

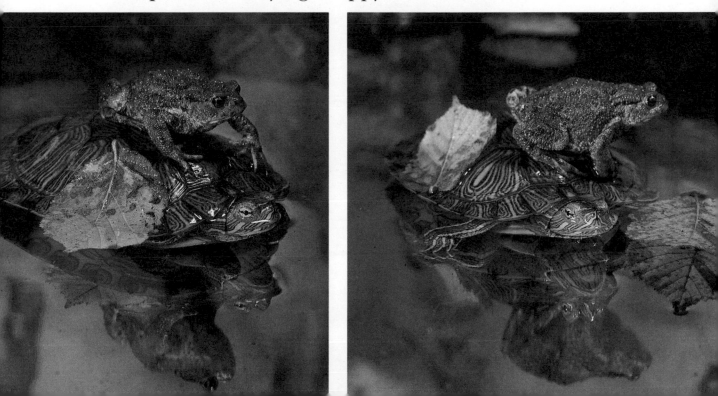

Two years old

Warm days in spring wake Hoppy out of her second hibernation. She makes her home in an empty flowerpot.

Emma the puppy meets her early one evening and bounces around her, wanting to play. She picks Hoppy up, but the toad oozes poison from her skin and Emma spits her out at once. Hoppy crawls home unhurt, but Emma foams at the mouth and shakes her head, trying to get rid of the awful taste of toad.

One day Hoppy feels dry and thirsty. She starts across the lawn, heading for the garden pond.

Oops! Hoppy almost steps on a grass snake basking in the sun. Grass snakes eat toads! Hoppy is very alarmed. She stands on tiptoe and puffs herself up with air. But the snake is only a small one, and Hoppy looks enormous, all puffed up. The snake is just as frightened of Hoppy and quickly slithers away.

In the pond Hoppy has a long drink, but not through her mouth. She sits on a lily pad and absorbs the water through her skin.

All through her third summer Hoppy eats and grows. She snaps up every small creature that comes her way in the night. When she meets a beetle grub crawling along, she watches it to be sure it is good toad food. She concentrates, staying absolutely still.

Suddenly—*zap!* Hoppy's pink tongue shoots out. In a split second the grub is caught on the sticky tip of her tongue and flipped into her mouth.

By autumn Hoppy is full grown. For the third time she goes into hibernation.

Three years old

Hoppy is out of hibernation and on the move again. She starts to crawl toward the big pond where she was born. Now that she is grown up, she is ready to spawn. Other adult toads are crawling toward the pond too.

Hoppy has a long, long way to crawl, but
nothing can stop her. She climbs walls, hops out
of ditches, scrambles along the ground. She
even has to cross a busy road. Cars hurtle by,
their headlights glaring. But Hoppy crosses
safely. At last she reaches the pond and
splashes in.

Bert, who is much smaller than Hoppy, swims
over to her and climbs onto her back. Hoppy
lays her spawn in the water. Bert covers it with
a fluid called sperm so that the eggs can hatch.

Hoppy has finished spawning. She rests awhile, then leaves the pond. Most mother toads don't take care of their eggs or tadpoles. Slowly Hoppy makes her way back to her flowerpot home for the summer.